To:

Marg Christians

From:

Avery St. Church Coffee-Break

Date:

May 12, 2003

Message:

Thanks for always being so willing to play the piano. You always add that special touch to our Monday Night Coffee-Break !! :) love, Anne

Rise and Shine

Alma Barkman

MOODY
The Name You Can Trust®
A MINISTRY OF MOODY BIBLE INSTITUTE

RISE AND SHINE by Alma Barkman

© 1999:   Christian Art
          PO Box 1599
          Vereeniging
          1930
          South Africa

This book was first published in the United States by Moody Press with
the title of *Rise and Shine*, copyright © 1986 by the Moody Bible
Institute of Chicago.

Designed by: Christian Art

ISBN 08024-4751-1

Printed in Singapore.

Day one

A voice is calling, "Clear the way for the Lord".
Isaiah 40:3

They're off to school! And here I stand in the aftermath, wondering where to begin. The back step is littered with mismatched socks, outdated shoes, and a jacket that never *did* fit.

Inside the door are an onion for today's soup and a tub full of cucumbers with a thatch of dill weed on top for tomorrow's pickles. The sink is piled high with dirty dishes from last night's potluck supper. Coffee mugs and cereal bowls clutter the kitchen table, and school lists, report cards, spare textbooks, and sandwich crumbs are strewn on the counter top. Somebody has left his lunch money beside the cactus plant but thoughtfully placed a pound of margarine in the sun so it would soften.

It has.

Meanwhile the tomcat has upset his dish, walked

through the contents, and is grooming himself in the middle of an unmade bed. Where do I begin?

With a good, strong cup of coffee, for one thing. I rinse out a cup and pull up a chair. Ah! The first ten-minute solitude in two long months – and the doorbell has to ring. Pride tells me not to answer, but conscience urges me on.

"I can see you're just in the middle of cleaning," says my neighbor, spying the mop that has been leaning against the wall since yesterday. Her gracious oversight eases my embarrassment and serves as a clue to her understanding ways. I invite her in. Not the least disturbed by the condition of my house, she clears a place for herself at the table and joins me for coffee.

After she is gone I resume my "cleaning" with renewed enthusiasm. Her presence has boosted my morale.

When God comes to the doorstep of my day, do I invite Him in? Or am I too self-conscious about the clutter in my life? Sometimes I sense His presence as an embarrassing inconvenience. I want time to clean up this habit or correct that fault, and *then* I will honor Him with a special invitation to join me.

But God is a Friend who understands the frustrations and failures of a disorganized life. He comes to me with just the encouragement I need to straighten my values and put my spiritual house in order.

Rise: Read 1 Corinthians 10:13 and Revelation 3:20

Shine: Reassure someone who is struggling with a similar problem with a reminder that he is not alone. By "opening up" the moral clutter of our lives to an understanding God, we can find new purpose and meaning in life.

First aid

He has sent me to bind up the brokenhearted.
Isaiah 61:1

Although not a registered professional, I do get my share of nursing experience, particularly while substituting for the school secretary. The minute I set foot inside the door, casualties start gravitating toward the office – scraped elbows, skinned knees, old wounds, fresh nosebleeds, raised toenails, broken blisters, upset stomachs.

I have learned that a school secretary opens a well-stocked first-aid kit long before sharpening any pencils. By midafternoon the office is apt to resemble a hospital ward.

Not only that, but old Florence Nightingale is not accorded any degree of privacy. The casualty victims from school are beginning to spill over into my house. Yesterday the doorbell rang, and a terrified young fellow

9

hopping up and down on my doorstep tried to tell me that his pal was bleeding to death on the road – massive hemorrhage.

I ran to the site of the accident, where the victim was just untangling himself from the wreckage of his bicycle. Judging from his groans, I thought he had amputated his leg.

Somehow I managed to get him into my bathroom and wash off his wounds. An accurate diagnosis confirmed my suspicions: he had simply scraped the scab from a previous injury. I solemnly conjured up an impressive-looking bandage, and he was back on the road in no time at all, completely cured.

The therapeutic value of Band-Aids may well be disputed, but this is one "lady of the lamp" who keeps her medicine chest well stocked.

Whether it is a tiny sliver in a chubby finger, or cancer clawing at a ravaged frame, pain demands priority. Why then am I so hesitant in dispensing consolation? Do I wait until an emergency demands it before investing in a "first-aid" kit? Must I first suffer physically, mentally, emotionally, or spiritually before I learn the healing value of a soothing hand, a mutual tear, a sympathizing heart, an understanding word?

Surely I do well to keep my medicine chest well stocked with love and compassion as well as with bandages, for I never know when I will be called upon to deal with tragedy, or when tragedy may call to deal with me.

Rise: read Luke 10:30-37. Think back to the last time you were in pain physically, emotionally, or spiritually. Who was your "Good Samaritan"? How did he help the most when you were hurting?

Shine: Let someone know you care. Remember him with a phone call, a card, or a visit.

Snared

And forgive us our debts.
Matthew 6:12

$\mathcal{I}$ got tangled up in one of those gigantic sale days at a large shopping center this morning and thought I would have to spend the night there. Shopping carts were heaped high with everything from light bulbs to salted peanuts, and every second cart had two or three furnace filters tilted at right angles to the wind. Those who had bypassed the convenience of a shopping cart lamented their lack of foresight as they tried to peek over thirteen rolls of toilet tissue balanced on an armload of paper towels.

As time dragged by at the checkouts, mothers had their hands full trying to discourage toddlers from shoplifting everything in sight, and desperate young fathers tried to assuage the thirst of squawling infants, most of whom had long ago decided that sale day was not their cup of tea. More mobile kids had taken off on their own steam and so, crammed between announcements pleading for more cashiers and the garbled details of the latest blue-light special, were frantic reports of lost progeny.

I was fortunate. I was alone. I had what I wanted, and I had it in a shopping cart. My one concern was to get home before supper. Oh, my feet were complaining, and I wished I had tucked a camp stool into my purse, but otherwise I was doing rather well.

The most ironic part of the whole deal was that nobody ahead of me was paying cash. It was credit cards all the way. I came home convinced that the economy must be in bad shape if people have to buy toilet tissue on time.

But credit is like that. It lures us like flies into the glistening web of affluence, and even though we are the victims of our own indulgence, we still have the audacity to blame the spider for trespassing.

Will we never learn that by its very nature, the god of materialism is out to snare us and suck us dry, to drain our resources and consume all our time? Perhaps that is why in the Lord's Prayer repentance ("forgive us our debts") is sandwiched between our needs ("give us this day our daily bread") and our wants ("lead us not into temptation"). God alone knows how gullible we really are.

Rise: Read Psalm 23. Is it not in sharp contrast to the commercialism of our times?

13

Shine: Divide your shopping lists into "needs" and "wants." Has the dividing line become blurred? To avoid temptation, leave your credit cards at home for a week, a month, a year. By deliberately curbing your wants, help fulfill the real financial needs of someone else.

The building permit

*For every house is built by someone,
but the builder of all things is God.
Hebrews 3:4*

𝒴ou know how kids are. Why, to let our young son tell it, the housing shortage for birds is so critical we dare not wait until suppertime – when father will be home – to start the construction of a birdhouse. We have to build one right away or the wrens will be forced to take up residence in someone else's yard.

Reluctantly I agree to help, but only under certain conditions. Do we have sufficient wood?

"Yep!" In no time at all Junior is back with enough used lumber for a toolshed.

Does he know where to find the saw?

"Yep!" Right over there in the crotch of the maple tree. He left it there when he built his tree house last fall. What about nails? No problem. He proudly presents me with a soup can full of rusty spikes. There remains just one ray of hope in an otherwise grim situation.

"What if I can't drill the hole?"

Alas, he has thought about that too.

"Oh, I've got this neat board with a knothole already in it. I've been keeping it under my bed." (Just like his father – always insists you should sleep over a problem.)

He returns with the piece of wood, and it does, indeed, have a knothole the appropriate size for wrens. Still trying to squirm out of the ordeal confronting me, I present the only remaining argument.

"Look," I point out, "the knothole isn't even in the middle."

He looks at it rather thoughtfully for a long time and then says, "Do you suppose the wrens would know the difference?"

I know when I'm stumped, so we make the birdhouse. Lopsided and shaky, it hangs in the backyard where wrens for generations to come will sing the praises of one small boy's persistence. Every time I hear them I'll flinch, knowing how useless it is to try and thwart God's people if it's God's plan.

I can hedge about the inconvenience of their demands and say I haven't time to help – when I do. I can demand certain prerequisites and say they haven't been met – when they have. I can set unrealistic standards and say they're vital – when they're not. But if the project is ordained of God, and I am obedient to His will, He will

16

draw me in despite myself, a reluctant builder blessed beyond belief.

Rise: Read Psalm 127

Shine: Your contribution to the kingdom of God may not be glamorous, but it has eternal purpose and significance. Ask God to keep you faithful in your commitment and trust Him to supply the needed grace, even when you feel the task is beyond you.

Cleaning stove pipes

*And the foundations of the thresholds trembled at the voice
of him who called out, while the temple was filling with
smoke. Then I said, "Woe is me, for I am ruined".*
Isaiah 6:4-5a

I can remember my mother fussing and fuming around
the old wood stove, declaring it was time to clean the
pipes again because the fire was sluggish. Dad always
dragged his feet about such matters, no doubt trying to
summon up enough vocabulary to match the occasion.

He succeeded admirably.

Just once I made the mistake of jiggling his ladder at
precisely the wrong moment. In a vain attempt to escape
the ear-splitting pandemonium that followed, my dog
went bounding through the soot and jumped up on the
new velour sofa, triggering off a second volley of rebukes
far more vociferous that the first.

As if the air wasn't already contaminated enough after

18

such a verbal explosion, my mother decided to paint the pipes. To this day I somehow think the fumes of that silver paint were meant to purge my impressionable young mind of any foul words that had recently lodged there. Gasping for fresh air, I hurried out into self-imposed exile, while my father sauntered sheepishly off to his machine shop, and mother embarked on stage two of her clean-up campaign.

All afternoon I harbored a secret dread of meeting my father at the supper table. Like Isaiah of old who found himself before the very presence of God, I was painfully aware of my own bungling weaknesses, especially when compared to that awesome figure whose stentorian tones could shake my whole universe and set me quivering in my childish shoes. To my utter relief, when supper came nobody mentioned a word about my past misdemeanors nor did anyone seem to mind, least of all my father.

As we breathed the incense of freshly waxed floors and spread the butter on a peace offering of crusty brown rolls, the fire snapped and crackled cheerfully in the kitchen stove, and I gradually relaxed in the warm reassurance that all had been forgiven. Indeed, when my father casually asked whether someone would be willing to let in the dog, I ran to oblige with unprece-dented eagerness: I was good for something after all!

Like the prophet purified by the burning coal, I have since experienced more profound moments when an overwhelming sense of unworthiness mysteriously vanished the minute I said to the God who called, "Here am I, send me."

Rise: Read Isaiah 6. Notice the apparent futility of the prophet's message as a whole but the seed of hope it implanted within a few.

Shine: Even though the Christian service you offer does not *appear* successful, "keep on keeping on" in obedience to the Lord's call. Despite your feelings of inadequacy, God can use you to impart love and hope to people otherwise untouched by the gospel.

The cost of
commitment

You owe to me even your own self as well.
Philemon 19b

$\mathcal{M}$y tomcat, having acquired a taste for eccentric menus, is not feeling up to par. The vet assures me, via telephone, that even so common a problem nevertheless requires appropriate medication, and can I drop by the clinic to pick up the pills?

I am greeted by a low, threatening *grrooowwwll* as a massive German shepherd springs out of the examining room. He is clearly annoyed with the world in general and vets in particular, but his main thrust is focused on a canine rival just entering the door behind me. Instantly I picture myself the hapless victim in a vicious round of barks and bites, but at a crucial moment the vet herself intervenes. She is a petite little lady who is obviously an

21

expert at directing the animal traffic that flows through her office. She bids farewell to the German shepherd, welcomes two cats, admires a poodle with painted toenails, and accompanies a lame collie into the examining room.

The outer door opens again, and in bounds a youthful Labrador. Instinctively sniffing the well-spotted rug, his intentions are abruptly thwarted by a sharp jerk on his leash, and he sits down reluctantly at his master's feet. Spontaneously jarred from their jealous contemplation of each other's pedigrees, the two cats rise simultaneously to do battle with this common foe, their snarls and hisses in turn provoking the poodle to all sorts of nervous expressions. Not a minute too soon, the vet reappears with the prescription for my tomcat.

Stretched out luxuriously across the bed at home, he is indifferent to the fact that I have just risked life and limb on his behalf. And being a proud feline, he probably figures he was worth every ounce of the sacrifice.

Annoyed by his lack of appreciation, I can't help but wonder how God feels about my own ingratitude. Even so common a problem as sin required a personal Mediator, One who ventured into this vile world and was hissed and spat upon by men not far removed from animals. If questioned, I would readily agree: I owe eternal life to Him. Yet reclining on a luxuriant bed of ease, my actions somehow contradict my words. Is it possible that, being a Christian, I take Christ's sacrifice too much for granted, convinced that He owes me far more than I owe Him?

Rise: Read Romans 12:1-8.

Shine: Is your commitment to Christ lagging in favor of leisure pursuits? Rededicate yourself to the Lord. Diligently exercise the gifts He has given you for His honor and glory.

Love letters

See with what large letters I am
writing to you with my own hand.
Galatians 6:11

They arrived at regular intervals by mail – little parcels done up in brown paper. We would open one to discover a length of homemade sausage, together with an explanatory note: "We butchered today on the farm. We wanted you to taste the sausage. Do not forget to enjoy it. Love, Mother."

A few weeks later the mailman would bring another package. As we unwrapped it a note would fall out. "We got some cream, so I made some butter. I froze it yet in the parcel so it would be just right when you get it." Her unlimited faith in Canada's postal system was always honored. The butter, though soft, still held its shape, and like most of the goodies she sent, it was simply rolled in the wax paper from cereal boxes, and neatly secured with an overstretched jar ring.

If a parcel rattled when we shook it, the little note might say: "The hens laid well this week. Here are some noodles I made." On special occasions she included "something for everyone." The aprons were always neatly pieced together from assorted prints and trimmed with bias tape. Tucked into the pocket was a bag of candy along with the familiar note: "The licorice, it is for Leo. The red hanky is for him to wipe his face when he eats it. I remem-ber how it got so black as he was small!" There would be other treats for the grandchildren – a mechanical rabbit, a toy car, a Bible story book, and always a little note written separately for each child.

As Grandma grew older, the parcels were fewer and farther between, but the letters continued, the handwriting large, the words a bit shaky, but messages of love nonetheless, painstakingly conveyed by a mother's hand.

In this age of computerized mailing lists and form letters, I tell myself that typing is far more legible and phoning so much faster than writing a few affectionate lines to friends and loved ones. But sometimes in among the bills and the formal business letters and the junk mail, I find a note personally addressed to me in curious handwritten scrawl. As I contemplate which saint has taken time to write I catch a glimpse of teacher, preacher, traveler Paul – afflicted, persecuted, imprisoned, yet through it all a faithful scribe, and suddenly I know again the value of epistles penned in love.

Rise: Read 2 Corinthians 3:2-3.

Shine: Be aware that your loving presence has a special impact in an impersonal world. Let the love of God flow through your pen to touch lonely hearts wherever they may be.

Providing insight

*And this is the will of Him who sent Me, that
of all that He has given Me I lose nothing.*
John 6:39

Our son wears contact lenses. In water they look like
bubbles cut in half. Very small bubbles. One-half inch
in diameter, to be exact.

This morning the phone rings. Very early. "Uh – Mom
– are you awake? Mom? Mom?"

I can hear saws and hammers banging and buzzing in
the background, and I wonder if I still have a son in the
carpentry shop with all ten fingers. No, he hasn't sawn
one off. He's lost a contact lens. No, not in the sawdust.
At home, in the bathroom, just before leaving for work.
Will I go see if I can find it?

So I am soon down on the floor of the bathroom,
rubbing the sleep from my own eyes and squinting
around under the sink for a half-inch bubble cut in half.

I comb every inch of the room and am shuffling out the door when my slipper kicks aside a brittle piece of plastic. I pick it up with the intention of tossing it into the garbage, but as I hold it in my hand it begins to come to life, or I wake up, or both. Whatever happens, I realize it is the lost contact lens, so shriveled and curled it resembles a piece of dried cellophane tape.

I cradle it in my hand and head for the phone. In no time at all the youthful owner is on the other end of the line giving me lengthy and detailed instructions on how to rejuvenate a hundred dollars' worth of eye equipment. And stroking my empty wallet, I am listening very, very carefully.

Once in a while I meet a person who confides that she is interested in Christian writing. She believes, according to 1 Corinthians 12:7, that God may have equipped her to serve Him in this special way, but the gift seems so minute, the prospects of uncovering it so farfetched, that she solicits my help.

Her aspirations may be vague, her aptitude not that apparent, but the sincerity of her appeal cannot be ignored. Feeling very much at a loss, I feel I must drop to my knees on her behalf and ask Christ to use me in broadening her vision. Under the providence of God, something usually "clicks," and both of us are blessed with a clearer perspective and divine guidance. Aware of the responsibility involved, both of us must be sensitive to the direction provided.

Rise: Read 1 Corinthians 12:1-11.

Shine: Seek out and encourage those people whose gifts may not be as obvious to them as they are to you. Your words may help open up new avenues of service for one of God's children.

The ultimate resource person

No good thing does He withhold from those who walk uprightly. O Lord of hosts, how blessed is the man who trusts in thee.
Psalm 84:11

We come home late, and I'm busy bustling the kids off to bed when the youngest stops short in his tracks, turns pale, and says, *"I forgot!"*

"Forgot *what*?" I ask impatiently.

"I forgot – *(sniff!)* – I forgot – my labels."

"What labels?"

"The labels for social studies. I need stuff – *(sniff, blow)* – I need labels from stuff that comes from here and stuff that comes from somewhere else."

"You mean food?"

"Yeah, food. From Canada and from somewhere else."

"Ok, everybody. We gotta help this guy find some labels. I'll look in here. Somebody else look on that shelf." In no time at all the cupboards are bare, but the kitchen is crowded – crowded with cans and boxes and bags and labels. Somebody is debating the origin of pineapples and somebody else is cutting the side out of a carton of rice, and our little geography student is sitting calmly in the midst of it all assessing which would be the prettiest labels to glue into his notebook.

For some strange reason I am not even that annoyed with him. I guess I remember the time when I was his age and the teacher told us to bring a picture of a cow. All the way home I pondered where I would find that picture. And I got home, and I forgot all about it.

About two in the morning I awoke with a bang! The cow! I've forgotten the picture of the cow! So I tiptoed into my mother's room and woke her up to tell her of my plight. By the light of the old coal-oil lamp the two of us started going through the pile of newspapers. No cows. We tried the catalog. One cow. She was standing behind the chain link fencing that Eaton's used to advertise. But she was not a very *nice* cow. The tears started to overflow, and I was shivering with the cold, and my mother said, "Let's go and make some cocoa." And she opened the cupboard door and there was a COW! The nicest, neatest cow you have ever seen, pictured on the side of the Cow Brand Baking Soda box. Without a moment's hesitation, Mom dumped the soda into a bowl, grabbed the scissors, and cut out my cow. And I got an "A plus" on my lesson.

I have relived that experience dozens of times, vividly remembering the feelings of utter hopelessness that overwhelmed me in the middle of that dark night and the awful reluctance to wake my mother. And then there was the disturbing realization that I would have to settle for second best. But finally, just when morale was lowest, I experienced the pure joy of seeing, right before my eyes, the answer to my need.

The secret of that joy lay in discovering the right source. Unless I "delight myself in the Lord," unless I open the door to His provisions for my life, He will never give me the "desires of my heart." In fact I have only a hazy concept of what those desires really are, yet God is able to provide "exceedingly abundantly beyond all that we ask or think" (Ephesians 3:20).

Rise: Read Acts 17:24-27.

Shine: Encourage someone who is at the end of his resources to open his heart to the abundant life in Christ Jesus.

A stinging rebuke

God has chosen the foolish things
of the world to shame the wise.
1 Corinthians 1:27

A fine fat bumblebee has taken up residence under our back step, but being short-sighted, he usually touches down just a few inches short of his runway. Mumbling and grumbling he toddles about looking for the entrance to his hive, and having found it, he waddles in under the concrete step with his load of nectar. A few seconds later he reappears, adjusts his "bee-focals," revs his motor, and takes off.

In spring he drones on and on about the tulips blooming late. Then all the fruit trees blossom at once, and he has to fly overtime. Then along comes a bumper crop of dandelions.

Fascinated by the bee's bumbling antics, I mark out his runway by planting posies at my doorstep. Every time I watch a black and yellow bee hovering over purple petunias, I have to marvel. Scientists claim a bumblebee should not be able to fly. His body is too big. His wings are too short. His fuzz creates too much drag. In short, he violates the very laws that make flight possible. But while the experts puzzle over the impossible design of his fuselage, the bumblebee zooms off time and again into the great blue yonder.

Because human wisdom comes to depend on all sorts of logical explanations, God in His super-natural insight occasionally stirs us from complacency by breaking His own rules. If the fact that a bumblebee can fly seems too insignificant to attract much attention, God can always dribble molten lava down a mountain or tickle up an earthquake, rattling the Richter scale at will and forcing our puny minds to concede to a Power so much greater than ourselves.

"'My thoughts are not your thoughts, neither are your ways, my ways,' declares the Lord" (Isaiah 55:8). Is that not why scientists are baffled that a force as strong as love cannot be measured in a test tube? And why advocates of faith by works are stymied that God should send His Son incarnate to the cross? Whether for the aviator observing a bumblebee in flight, or for the experts researching the field of physics, or for skeptics probing the realm of spiritual renewal, it would seem that God has indeed chosen the foolish things of the world to shame the wise and "the weak things of the world to shame the things which are strong" (1 Corinthians 1:27).

Puzzled and perplexed, the mind may seek for explanations, but the searching soul finds God.

Rise: Read Isaiah 55:6-13.

Shine: The next time someone expresses his bewilderment at a strange turn of events, suggest that God may be the moving force behind it.

Actions speak louder

*I have inclined my heart to perform
Thy statutes forever, even unto the end.
Psalm 119:112*

Friend Hubby, delving around for ideas to use with his Sunday school class, decides to take some dramatic action.

"For your information," he declares rather grandly, "we are going to act out the story of the Israelites wandering in the wilderness."

"And who, pray tell, is going to play the part of Moses?"

"He standeth before you."

"Pardon me. I didn't recognize him."

"That's precisely my problem. I need a costume."

And so at 11:00 P.M. on Saturday night I am outfitting Moses for his forty year sojourn – Grandma's cane, an old green bathrobe, some cast-off sandals. "And be sure

36

to take off your glasses. Moses' eye was not dimmed, remember?"

"But his stomach got empty. What do we use for manna?"

"Let's see, it was round and white – and – popcorn! That's it! Popcorn manna."

"And the quails?"

"This old plastic parrot would do."

Sunday morning I get up to pop the manna while friend Hubby gathers up his costume. "You're sure you have everything now?"

"Yep!" replies Moses. "I've got the manna if you've got the quail."

We are met by curious stares as we enter the church with our props and paraphernalia. People of lesser imagination do not realize that this is the memorable occasion on which a certain Sunday school class wanders in the wilderness with Moses, feasting on popcorn and parrot as they journey to the Promised Land.

When I stop to think about it, all the world is a theater in the round, each of us simultaneously involved in a lifelong production. A review of my Christian performance in the light of 1 Corinthians 13 is not very flattering to the ego: oratory dry, showmanship shallow, sacrifice worthless.

It appears that mastering the script means more than memorizing the lines and then waiting for the curtain to go up. It's living the way the Author intended, backstage, in the kitchen, the office, the classroom, where impromptu gestures of faith, hope, and love do not bring standing ovations, just "Well done, thou good and faithful servant."

Rise: Read Psalm 100.

Shine: In what ways would you like to serve the Lord more creatively? Ignore the critics and give the Director the best performances of your life. The applause comes later.

Be on guard

And a trap snaps shut on him.
Job 18:9

$\mathcal{J}$ am substituting for the school secretary when a brown-eyed young rascal comes into the office with a bag of marbles.

"Want to see how many I've got?" He loosens the drawstring of the bag, and just as I peer in, out pops a white mouse.

Now contrary to what people may expect, I am not afraid of mice. "Herman" and I get along just fine. I hold him in my hand and admire his fine pink eyes while he shows me how fast he can quiver his whiskers. We pop him back into the bag just as the principal walks by, and the learned gentleman is none the wiser.

He does not have a very perceptive nose.

Anyone who has grown up in an old rural farmhouse can detect the presence of a mouse just by sniffing around a bit. They give off a peculiar musty odor. I can remember my mother saying, "There's a mouse in the house. I can smell it," and out came the cheese and trap.

Now there was no better spectator sport than keeping vigil at a mousetrap. I would pull up my chair, wrap myself in a patchwork quilt, turn down the wick of the old coal-oil lamp, and wait.

Shadows flickered and danced on the wallpaper, entertaining my active imagination with all sorts of interesting creatures. As the lamp chimney darkened with soot the dragons grew larger and larger until eyes heavy with sleep could no longer distinguish their outlines. Then suddenly – SNAP!

The trap would go off, and I'd spring to my feet and dash off to bed, never once looking back to see what I'd caught. My mother could have that privilege!

Even as an adult I find I am still intrigued by real-life suspense. As a result, small bits of gossip can chew their way past my better judgment and completely captivate my thoughts. I am wrapped up in the harmless (?) pastime of piecing them together, the light of godly discernment gradually grows dim. Suspicions multiply. Conjecture grows. Supposition expands. And then I read: "For as he thinketh in his heart, so is he" (Proverbs 23:7, KJV*).

Snap!

The trap goes off. Seeing myself for what I really am, I spring to my senses and seek the Lord's forgiveness.

Contrary to what I would like to believe, Christians

are easily enticed into the spectator sport of gossip, and yet, when confronted by a guilty conscience, I am just as apt to run the other way, too cowardly to cope with the consequences, even though I enjoyed the "entertainment."

Are you that way too?

Rise: Read Proverbs 26:20-28.

Shine: Pray with David in Psalm 141:3: "Set a guard, O Lord, over my mouth; keep watch over the door of my lips."

* *King James Version.*

Casting for souls

Your tackle hangs slack.
Isaiah 33:23

One cork, a fishhook, a length of shop cord, a few worms tossed into a tin can, and I had all the makings of a good afternoon's entertainment. Half the enjoyment was rounding up the fishing tackle. The cork was usually an old cast-off salvaged from somebody's broken thermos bottle, the fishhook a rusty one hidden on an attic windowsill, and the "sinker" an outsized washer from Dad's collection of nuts and bolts.

I hoped my mother would go shopping any day now and come home with a goodly sized parcel tied with string. If not, I could always accompany her to town and stand there wistfully eyeing that huge ball of shop cord until the grocer took the hint and whacked off a piece long enough for a fish line. I always took time to thank him profusely, for I never knew when a whale might snap my line and I'd need another piece of string to replace it.

My older brother was the one to approach concerning a pole. He not only handled an ax, but he was also pretty adept with his jackknife when it came to peeling a green willow.

Earthworms were plentiful in the garden plot, even if I had to shoo away the flock of hens who gobbled up my prospective bait as fast as I uncovered it.

At last everything was assembled, and I headed toward the creek in my bare feet. I loved to go fishing! Along the path the fiddlehead ferns were uncurling in the shade of giant elms, and wild violets nodded shyly as I passed by. Water bugs sprinted across a quiet pool at the river's edge, and a bullfrog dozed in a blast-off position on his lily-pad launch.

A fallen tree provided a comfortable seat right over the fishing hole, and I settled into its branches, dropped my line into the water, and unfolded the brown paper bag containing my lunch. The sun was warm on my back, the breeze gentle. I was blissfully beyond the reach of worldly cares, yet alert to the slightest nibble.

The irony of the situation was that the fellow upstream who envied me my "luck" owned an expensive rod and reel, which he found too complicated to use. Similarly frustrated, some of the best-equipped fishers of men never get a bite, while their barefoot cousins stagger Home at sunset with a satisfied smile and a string of souls to their credit.

I can only conclude that a "tackle" box bulging with all sorts of spiritual lures is sometimes too awkward to carry along the narrow path that leads to the old fishing hole of lost souls. Cumbered down by methods and means, it is easier simply to forfeit the opportunity than to go out on a limb in reaching others for Christ.

Rise: Read John 21:3-6.

Shine: Perhaps your "fishing" has not been fruitful because you are holding too rigidly to a prescribed method and overlooking the people you want to "catch". Try another approach. Forget everything you ever knew about "fishing" and just launch out into the deep, using whatever resources you have handy.

Understanding
what we read

Be diligent to present yourself approved to
God as a workman who does not need to be
ashamed, handling accurately the word of truth.
2 Timothy 2:15

There is no escape.

The minute before you are born, an admitting clerk at the hospital pushes a sheet of paper across the desk and says to your mother, "You'll have to fill this form out first, please."

Three days later you are bawling your little bald head off because Mom won't take time to feed you. She has to fill out a form for the vital statistics people.

Once you are duly named and registered, surely she'll have time for more important things. She does. She turns around and fills out a form for the family allowance

45

payments. With an appetite like yours, she figures she needs all the subsidies she can get, forms or no forms.

Six-week check-up – fill out a form.

Booster shots at the local health clinic – fill out a form.

First visit to the dentist – fill out a form.

Register for kindergarten – fill out another form.

And that's only the beginning. Mothers, bless their hearts, sign their lives away on permission slips, consenting, conceding, agreeing, approving, acknowledging, promising, and whatever else they do when they fill out forms and sign their names to stuff nobody ever bothers to read.

And so the other day it was refreshing to discover that I had inadvertently entered our son in a Herbie contest. At least that's what he claimed. He even began to wonder if he'd win.

"What's the prize?" I asked.

"I dunno. You signed the paper."

"I did? What did it look like?"

"About so big. My teacher said to bring it right back cuz it was 'portant."

I began to wonder what I'd signed. I kept on wondering. Right until five o'clock I wondered. And then as I started to make supper my daughter shoved a form in amongst the potato peelings.

"Here, Mom. You're supposed to sign this."

Up piped her kid brother. "That's it! That's it! That's the form about the Herbie contest. See, it says right here

–" and he poked around with a grubby finger until he'd located the right words – "See, it says 'Herbie contest.'"

That's what he *thought* it said. Oh, well, everybody makes mistakes. "Hereby consent" *does* look a lot like "Herbie contest," don't you agree? I thought so.

When it comes to interpreting Scripture we can just as easily be led astray. Just because a passage seems to us to have a certain meaning does not necessarily make it so. The more familiar it is the less attention we are apt to pay to it. All the while we may actually be deceiving ourselves.

The importance of sound teaching by authoritative people who are respected figures in the historic Christian faith cannot be overemphasized. I can be very sincere in my personal Bible study, but I also run the risk of being sincerely *wrong*.

Rise: Read 2 Peter 1:16-21.

Shine: Approach a familiar portion of Scripture and read it as if for the very first time. Is its meaning exactly the same for others as it is for you? Find out. You may be in for some surprises.

Adjustments

Restore to me the joy of Thy salvation.
Psalm 51:12

Things are quiet this morning.

The rag dolls are chucked in a corner of her bedroom, and the stuffed animals abandoned in favor of live playmates. The beach thongs are tossed in the closet and the play clothes thrown aside on a chair. The gym shoes are gone, and the hanger that held the new set of clothes is bare. A half-open desk drawer is empty of notebooks and pencils, and the tomcat sleeps undisturbed in the center of her unmade bed. Her alarm clock ticks rather loudly today.

In the bathroom the toothbrush is still damp, the tube freshly squeezed. The soap is unusually soft and gooey from prolonged use, and the washcloth, awkwardly wrung out by small hands, is drip, drip, dripping a puddle onto the bathroom floor.

As I pass the living room I notice that a scruffy toy dog has been perched in front of the TV for company, and they stare at one another with blank looks. I follow a trail of scattered clothes into our son's room, where a black plastic kite is draped haphazardly over the top of his dresser. Blue jean cut-offs lie on the floor beside his baseball glove, mute evidence that another summer has passed. Up on the windowsill a tomato from his very own garden is ripening in the sun, and out in the driveway a battered old wagon loaded with corn husks is still hitched to his bicycle, waiting for four o'clock. Yes, school has just begun, and things are quiet today.

Childish squabbling throughout the long hot months of summer, the frustrating lack of purpose and routine, the constant complaints about boredom no longer fill the major portion of my day. I am free – free to think, to order my affairs rightly, to spend my time as I see fit, unencumbered by the responsibilities of a family under-foot. I had often yearned for this day. At times I had even prayed for it! But now that it is here I am strangely disillusioned. The exhilaration of launching into a totally new life-style has ebbed a little. The friendly exchanges with neighbors have dwindled, now that the children no longer demand our mutual attention. In short, I have more adjustments to make than I had anticipated.

The same is also true for the new Christian. The turmoil and unrest that fill so much of an unbeliever's life can lift very suddenly when he comes to faith in

Christ. And even though he welcomes the prospects of inner peace, little reminders of the past keep tugging at his heart. The joy of his salvation may ebb. The community of caring Christians may not be as attentive. He may suddenly feel alone.

No doubt about it. For the new believer, there are adjustments to be made, new pursuits to follow, new people to befriend, but there is also time to deepen his relationship with the Lord.

Rise: Read Philippians 3:13-21.

Shine: Approach someone you feel may be having trouble adjusting to a Christian way of life. Help in any way you can to guide him into the abundant life.

Taking time

Finally, brethren, whatever is true, whatever is honorable, whatever is right, whatever is pure, whatever is lovely, whatever is of good repute, if there is any excellence and if anything worthy of praise, let your mind dwell on these things.
Philippians 4:8

Family vacations are so tightly scheduled these days I feel sorry for the children. They are so busy they have no time to tame a squirrel or watch a woodpecker or follow a garter snake.

They have no time to see a spider spin her web or a bumblebee visit a snapdragon or a humming-bird hover at a carragana.

They have no time to track a mother cat to see where she has hidden her kittens in the hollow log or crawl through a hayloft to find a hen's nest or chin themselves on a maple limb to peek at a robin's egg.

Children have no time to go barefoot on the damp cool mud of a coulee looking for fiddlehead ferns or slosh through the marsh in search of wild marigolds or sneak into the shady recesses along the river to watch a bullfrog.

They have no time to find wild violets growing beside the old hay rake or pink lady slippers in the gully.

They have no time to run through mud puddles in their bare feet or race the dog down the lane or swing out over the river on a rope.

They have no time to dangle their feet from a wooden bridge or catch dozens of minnow fish or build sand castles with a tin cup.

They have no time to watch a giant anthill or go picking berries just for fun or make a hammock between two trees.

No, there isn't time to daydream, to keep abreast of nature, or to sleep beside a strawstack. Quality of living has been replaced by quantity of life. The more ground our children cover, the more we think they learn. Exposure is good for them, we say. But exposure to *what*? Competition in the playground, destruction on the highways, evolution in the science courses, violence on TV, immorality in the neighborhood? And yet children are born with a different viewpoint. Romans 1:19-20 says, "For the truth about God is known to them instinctively; God has put this knowledge in their hearts. Since earliest times men have seen the earth and sky and all God made and have known of his existence and great eternal power" (TLB*).

Let's not quench that knowledge in our children. Let's cultivate it. Give them *time* to investigate the great mysteries of God. Deepen their understanding of Him through nature. Broaden their comprehension of a loving Creator. Remember that Christ said, "Consider the lilies." Don't crush them underfoot in your haste to have a "good" holiday.

Rise: Read Ecclesiastes 12:1-7.

Shine: Refrain from scheduling family times too tightly. Allow a leisurely investigation at close range of anything that captures your children's fancies. Take pleasure in their discoveries.

* *The Living Bible.*

Behind the scenes

Not even when one has an abundance
does his life consist of his possessions.
Luke 12:15b

*G*iven half a chance, kids can dredge up enough junk to
stock a surplus store. The annual Art and Science Fair
provides that chance. Balloons, spools, super glue, balsa
wood, teakettles, muskrat hides, dishpans of vermiculite,
thermometers, slabs of foam insulation, a squirrel tail,
jars, rubber bands, nails, bread pans, wood, string,
hammers, magazines, scissors, screwdrivers – the house
is suddenly reeling with frenzied activity.

Down in the basement we have the Wright brothers,
circa 1980, desperately building an air-plane before zero
hour.

Up in the dining room we have a trapper assembling
her supply of furs.

In the living room "Spike" Jones, alias Barkman, is

concocting an instrument from nails and rubber bands, using a bread pan as an amplifier.

In the kitchen the scientist is testing the effectiveness of insulation while standing ankle deep in foam chips and scratching like a monkey in fiberglass.

And down at the supermarket, old Mom is down on her hands and knees, pleading for another card-board box.

But nothing ever works. The plane is too heavy. The pelts shed their fur. The rubber bands snap. The thermometer lies. The cardboard boxes are *never* the right size.

So there is a mad stampede to the library for more ideas. In addition to the junk already accumulated, cast off, or recycled, there are now three dozen books scattered around the house that are either begged, borrowed, or overdue, yet none of which provide the exact information anyone needs.

Compound this confusion with a few grandiose schemes that are evidently spinoffs from a scientist's nightmare, throw in a case of stomach flu, add a few more cardboard boxes and a felt pen that runs dry at a crucial point, and you have only a faint idea of what goes on behind the scenes of the annual Art and Science Fair.

Parents with any insight whatsoever soon learn that the mark accorded is rarely, if ever, an accurate reflection of the student's true standing. The teachers grade only what they are shown. What they don't know about are all the failures that have been conveniently left behind. For every project completed, there are probably ten that were abandoned.

The same may be true of the person who tries to impress the world with his material goods. The outward appearance of affluence would indicate that here is a competent, highly successful man who truly knows where he is going. If the truth were known, he may be an anxious, frustrated individual who has left behind him a trail of broken dreams, abandoned hopes, and scattered plans.

As a Christian with insight I cannot judge only by what I see on the surface. Sometimes I must gently reach behind the facade of wealth and really see the person as he is. Those who "have it made" in one area can be falling apart in others.

Rise: Read Luke 12:16-21.

Shine: Think of someone you know who appears to be "laying up treasure for himself." Is he rich toward God? Tell him of the real riches he can have in Christ Jesus.

A stitch in time

*I looked for sympathy but there was none,
and for comforters, but I found none.*
Psalm 69:20b

*A*s dubious as it sounds, a cantankerous sewing machine can change a competent, self-composed woman into a sniveling, neurotic seamstress who sinks to her knees in despair at the drop of a stitch.

I can remember coming home with my arms draped in yard goods, visions of a brand new wardrobe drifting across the horizon of my dreams. Everything went beautifully until I sat down to sew. That's when the nightmare began.

Now the menfolk have to contend with such things as dirt in the carburetor of their car or water in the gas line or other such inconsequential nuisances. Once in a while they may even have to change the transmission, rebuild the motor, or some trivial little thing like that. But never,

ever, do they face the ordeal of trying to make a dress at the eleventh hour on a sewing machine that refuses to cooperate. The frustration is enough to reduce all but the most ingenious woman to a state of absolute despondency.

We had visitors from out of town recently, and they weren't inside the door before the woman handed me a partly finished dress she had been making. She never said a word, just stood there numb with despair, the half moons under her eyes betraying the time-consuming efforts she had put into it. Her husband, obviously bewildered by the strange transformation in his wife's personality, kept trying to apologize for her behavior. I recognized the symptoms at once. Closer examination of the unfinished dress revealed skipped stitches, irregular tension, puckered seams.

I advised him to buy her a new sewing machine.

"You mean to tell me that's her *only* problem?"

Suddenly she turned on him. "What do you mean, my *only* problem? Isn't that enough? Isn't it hard enough trying to sew in the first place besides having a machine that won't work? Isn't it bad enough that I have to sew during the night when nobody can see me cry and throw temper tantrums and act ridiculous just because of a stupid sewing machine? Isn't it enough that I've used more than I saved going from one place to another trying to get it adjusted? Isn't it —"

"There, there, dear," her husband interrupted.

"If you say so –"

"Don't say 'sew' to me!" she retorted. "I don't ever want to hear that word again!"

I knew exactly how she felt. I've been through it all myself. And whether there are frustrations caused by a cantankerous sewing machine or perplexing problems I face in my Christian walk, I can always rely on those who have struggled in similar areas to offer the best, most practical advice. In fact I believe that is why God allows me trials and testing – so that I can identify with those having similar needs and encourage them along the way.

Rise: Read 2 Corinthians 1:3-7.

Shine: Ask God to help you accept the fact that there is a greater purpose in hardships than what is immediately evident. Then share what you have learned with someone in similar straits.

More than
meets the eye

Do not judge according to appearance,
but judge with righteous judgment.
John 7:24

Oven mitts are like old hats. The longer you use them, the more reluctant you are to part with them. On the other hand, you don't want people to get the wrong impression, and so there you are – caught smack between common sense and social pressure.

I found myself the victim of such circumstances just the other day. We were to participate in a potluck supper. My contribution being a casserole, the thought occurred to me that I would have to transport a piping hot dish to church. It's the first time in ten years I have looked, really looked, at my oven mitts.

I believe they were green, once upon a time, trimmed

with yellow, perhaps. The years of service have tended to camouflage them. One thumb has been predominantly purple ever since I stuck it in the blueberry pie. The other thumb is caramel brown, for which I am grateful. Otherwise the syrup from the cinnamon buns would have caused third degree burns.

The palm of each oven mitt is beginning to stiffen a little with age, the padding having slipped to the middle (not exactly unusual, even in people). The resulting contour is a little bumpy and not altogether pleasing to the eye, so therefore I don't hang my oven mitts where they are subject to the stares of critical eyes, but tuck them away in a drawer. Even at that, I never slip them on without seeing the scorch mark where I accidently branded them on the red-hot element.

And now I was supposed to carry my casserole into church wearing *these* oven mitts? They looked so unap-petizingly bad I was concerned that people would be afraid to lift the cover of my dish. And so I bought myself a new pair, and that night I overheard one man say to another, "We'll just have to take our chances with this casserole. By the looks of those oven mitts, she's a brand-new cook."

With close to thirty years experience in the kitchen, I suddenly knew how Paul and his pal felt when they were regarded by the Corinthians as "deceivers and yet true" (2 Corinthians 6:8). I could scarcely refrain from pointing out to those skeptics that the casserole in question was mine and that I was not exactly a novice. In defending my dish, however, I could easily be accused of pride, so I kept my peace.

There have been other times when my best intentions have been misinterpreted, but I have discovered that people who are truly hungry for Christian fellowship do not jump to hasty conclusions. Overlooking apparent contradictions, they graciously dig deeper in order to fairly assess the circumstances from all angles.

Rise: Read 2 Corinthians 6:3-10.

Shine: Do you find it impossible to understand the behaviour of someone you know? Be charitable. Try to discover what is going on inside that person before passing comment.

Pass it on

*Now I praise you because you remember
me in everything, and hold firmly to the
traditions, just as I delivered them to you.*
1 Corinthians 11:2

$\mathcal{B}$ack in the days of our courtship, friend Hubby suggested I get the recipe for Jam Gem cookies from his mother. I duly inquired as to the ingredients, mixed up a batch, and proudly served them to him the next time he came to call.

"They are quite good," he remarked as he reached for seconds.

"Quite good" was not good enough. I tried again. And again. I could never solicit the kind of praise I hoped to hear.

It wasn't until long after we were married that he very sheepishly divulged the reason for his reserved comments. "Those cookies have to be a certain shape to taste

63

best."

"And what shape is that, pray tell?"

"Oval and about so big."

I went on a wild goose chase the likes of which uncovered every conceivable cookie cutter ever invented, but not one was "oval and about so big."

Months later I decided to confide in his mother. "Do you know," I whispered, "that your son insists that a genuine Jam Gem cookie has to be oval and about so big?"

She chuckled. "I suppose that's because I always made them that shape. Would you like my cookie cutter?"

I literally pounced on the offer. Wiping her hands on her apron, she pulled open a drawer and produced the elusive cookie cutter. It was the lid of a talcum powder can.

I have it still. The paint is worn off from prolonged use, and most people would consider it just another piece of junk, but my teenage daughter already has claimed it as an heirloom because it makes the best Jam Gems her dad has ever tasted.

I suppose every family has little traditions that are handed down from one generation to the next. The family of God is no exception. Those spiritual values that have shaped our lives are cherished and retained for the benefit of our children. Sometimes, like Grandma's cookie cutter, they are temporarily forgotten, tossed aside in the clutter of daily living.

But eventually a growing emptiness creates a hunger for the Christian principles that once guided us, the fellowship that church involvement provided us, the family devotions that once united us. And although we may not be aware of it, I believe the Holy Spirit uses our childhood memories to whet our appetite for the things of God. As we obediently search out His will and obey it, we in turn are establishing a Christian tradition for our children.

Rise: Read 2 Thessalonians 2:13-17.

Shine: As parents, maintain today those principles that you would like your children to inherit tomorrow.

Candid camera

And just as we have borne the image of the earthy,
we shall also bear the image of the heavenly.
1 Corinthians 15:49

$\mathcal{J}$ decided to start the New Year right by having my face lifted – the photographer promised to lift it from insignificance to fame with one shot. All I had to do was come in at the appointed hour.

Easier said than done. The streets were all ice. I don't believe I have skated on better. I was careening along the boulevard at the dizzy speed of five miles per hour, coming to rest crosswise at every stop sign. The male species was faring no better. For once there were no supercilious sneers emanating from behind their respective steering wheels. They were far too busy guarding their own fenders to worry about mine.

I arrived at the photographer's intact, or at least the car did. As for me, the sheer terror of so many close calls had permanently drained the blood from my face, my hair was standing on end, and I had proved beyond doubt the effectiveness of my super-dry deodorant.

The photographer was a little gnome with a chin whisker and flashing black eyes but no humor whatsoever. He pointed to the stool, and I wondered if this was how a convicted murderer goes to the gallows – heart palpitating, mouth dry, feet uncoordinated, hands trembling. He seemed to fiddle with the noose an awfully long time before he finally tripped the shutter. When he did, it was game over. No more posing. No fake smiles. The time for false pretenses had expired.

When I spread the proofs before the family, the teenager took one look and asked, "Do you think you might get home on parole, Mom?"

Although we chuckled at mug shots that show us in an unfavorable light, Scripture is deadly serious when it looks at our spiritual condition. Although God is merciful, He is also just. The unrepentant person who refuses to accept God's pardon through faith in Jesus Christ should not entertain ideas of going home to heaven "on parole." Despite the many and varied excuses, his sinful profile is unacceptable to a holy God. And although God is longsuffering, His Spirit will "not strive with man forever" (Genesis 6:3).

I can pose as a Christian. I can fake a Christian lifestyle. I can pretend to be everything I am not, but the moment of truth will come. "It is appointed unto men once to die, but after this the judgment" (Hebrews 9:27, KJV).

God knows every wrinkle. His spiritual camera "cannot lie" (Titus 1:2).

Rise: Read 1 John 1:5-10.

Shine: What picture do people have of you? Is it predominantly "earthly," or are you reflecting the grace of your heavenly Father? Read 1 John 1:9 again. Do what it says. Accept what is offered. Smile!

Shock value

That the power of Christ may dwell in me.
2 Corinthians 12:9

Years ago when we were building a house, we engaged the services of a recommended electrician. He drove an old panel truck, which came gasping up our driveway at sunrise, and I always debated what I would do with the thing if it sputtered and died on our doorstep.

After looking inside, I was even more concerned.

The upholstery had long ago rotted away, exposing the bare skeleton of the framework. The rib cage was crammed full of switches, circuit breakers, and coils of conduit. The owner had the habit of standing at the open door of his truck while baring wires, and the floorboards were carpeted with snips and scraps of copper threads and colored rubber shavings.

Somehow among the rubble he managed to locate sufficient materials to wire our house. Once in a while he had to come up from the basement to trace various circuits. I still haven't forgotten the day he stuck his screwdriver into a particular socket in the front room. The fire flew so far it shocked the life out of me and sent the tomcat skidding down the hallway.

Not the least bit alarmed, the old electrician slowly bent down to retrieve his screwdriver and remarked very matter-of-factly, "I guess it's live all right."

It was a good thing that screwdriver was well insulated, or I might not have been able to say the same for him.

In the Great Commission of Matthew 28:19-20, each of us is given a contract in which we are to take the good news of the gospel to people who are without spiritual power. Personally, I am so woefully inadequate at witnessing I am always afraid that when the opportunity knocks I may sputter and die on the doorstep. My courage ebbs, my brain becomes addled, I fidget for words. Crammed in among all the good intentions are the inconsistencies of disobedience and sin.

But Christ, who said, "I am with you always," is somehow able to sort through the clutter and extend His power through the most unlikely individuals. Sometimes, however, I become very complacent about spiritual matters, and He has to shock me back to reality. I believe that He exists; I talk of what He does; I see Him at work in others. It is in life's sudden jolts, however, that I personally comprehend His awesome power. As a Christian, I am not immune to tragedy and loss, but I

am insulated against despair. I am alive, all right –
eternally alive in Him.

Rise: Read Romans 12:1-3.

Shine: Perhaps you know someone who is
experiencing shocking upheavals in her life. Now is the
time to talk to her about Christ's power to help and to
heal.

Come and get it

And I will bring a piece of bread,
that you may refresh yourselves.
Genesis 18:5

$\mathcal{T}$he fellow who invented the automatic toaster probably thought he had averted a world crisis and that people would beat a path to his doorstep.

We did.

We came with every conceivable kind of bread but only about one piece in fifty met the specifications. The other forty-nine were either too thick or too moist or too big.

And so we turned sadly away, knowing that on the morrow we would have to resort to the same old *man*ual controls. And right in the midst of the morning turmoil, when the razor is buzzing, the kids are whining, and the teakettle's screaming, an ominous black cloud suddenly envelops the household. Everybody races toward the kitchen with arms flailing and accusations flying, and the poor fellow responsible flees for his own safety.

"The toast is burning – *again*!"

It is a phrase that has led to the breakdown of marriages, the upheaval of friendships, and the dissolution of sanity. It has interrupted solemn conversations, postponed major decisions, and created minor skirmishes. Its very utterance can shock a veteran, defeat a hardened warrior, and reduce a strong woman to tears. "The toast is burning!" plagues the conscience of the thrifty, condemns the lazy, and frustrates the busy. It deadens the hunger pangs of the starving, stifles the appetite of the sickly, and weakens the hearty. And why? Because that black pall of smoke is gruesome evidence that hope is gone. There is nothing left of our hot buttered toast but the charred remains of a broken dream. We may try, on the surface, to scrape away the damage, but the tinge of bitterness remains.

Hope in Christ is not like that. "I am the bread of life," He said. "He who comes to Me shall not hunger, and he who believes in Me shall never thirst" (John 6:35). Over the years those words have nurtured marriages, bonded friendships, and maintained sanity. They have been the topic of conversations, the pivot of major decisions, and the peacemaker in the midst of turmoil.

The words of Christ convinced the skeptics, softened rebellious hearts, and satisfied the spiritually hungry. They have eased the guilty conscience, encouraged the unwilling, and cautioned against anxiety. The empty have found fulfillment, the frail have found strengthening, and the spiritually dead have found eternal life. And why? Because Christ came that we might have life and that we might have it more abundantly. Instead of being continually "burnt up" by the shortcomings of men, we can depend upon the faithfulness of God. Which would you rather have – bitter black crumbs or hot buttered toast?

Rise: Read John 6:26-40.

Shine: The next time someone expresses disillusionment with life, challenge him to focus his hopes in Christ instead of in man.

Extending ourselves

*From the breath of God ice is made,
and the expanse of the waters is frozen.
Job 37:10*

The family had coaxed me all winter to go skating. I had always managed to find a way out of it – too busy, too tired, too cold, no skates. In their youthful innocence they never surmised the real reason – too *old*. I didn't even want to admit it to myself, so as a grand finale to winter, I took to the ice.

It never took to me.

It was just as cold and unyielding as ever.

Not about to be intimidated by a patch of frozen water, I swathed my bunions in three pairs of socks, laced up my borrowed blades, and inched toward the ice. My feet kept going faster than the rest of me. Before I knew it I was halfway across the pond – arms flailing like a windmill, feet rotating wildly. I must have looked like a

75

helicopter just touching down, and everybody scrambled up on the bank to see what would happen.

I latched onto a skating partner. It was a poplar tree that grew along the edge of the pond, and I shall ever be grateful for its unwavering support. Every time I felt my knees giving way, I would coast on my ankles as far as that tree and hang on for dear life, terrified that I would fall flat on my face if I let go. The family kept reminding me that skaters don't usually land on their *noses*. They are more apt to fall where they have more padding. I wasn't about to take chances.

I must have made at least two whole laps around the ice before calling it a day. By that time my legs were as supportive as two strands of spaghetti. Friend Hubby had laced my skates so tightly, I doubt if the blood will ever circulate beyond my kneecaps.

Next winter I think I will try to toboggan run instead. At least there, you are *expected* to sit down.

I once read a poem that expressed the idea that the soul must have its seasons. Whereas we find it easy to enjoy the jubilation of springtime, the exhilaration of summer and the rewards of autumn, the prospects of winter are chilly by comparison. We would much rather stay where we are comfortable and warm than lose dignity in some new venture. Afraid of adding credibility to the saying "There is no fool like an old fool," we cling to the familiar instead of coasting toward the supportive.

"Let go and let God" is just as applicable to the aging as it is to youth. So what if you flail around a bit at the beginning! You may also solicit some applause a little further down the ice. And if you find the challenge a bit too taxing, there are always other interests to pursue. The ice will melt, the spring will come, and you can go canoeing instead.

Rise: Read Isaiah 46:3-4.

Shine: Entice a senior citizen to participate in some new venture, thereby opening a door of opportunity that would otherwise remain closed.

The perfume of love

*And walk in love, just as Christ also loved
you, and gave Himself up for us, an offering
and a sacrifice to God as a fragrant aroma.*
Ephesians 5:2

On every side we are forced to defend ourselves
against a barrage of advertisements aimed at the body
beautiful. There are products guaranteed to smooth
wrinkles, moisten lips, curl eyelashes, soften toenails,
arch eyebrows, fatten hair, clean pores, harden finger-
nails, cover blemishes, and tighten flabbiness, thereby
dispelling any doubts we may have had about any part
of our anatomy. And deodorants are available to combat
any offensive odor the body is capable of producing.

There is but one remaining problem. In this highly
civilized, ultrasophisticated society, I am still stuck with
the same old nose. My olfactory organ threatens to revolt
every time it is bombarded by a horde of new fragrances

descending upon it, and yet there is no escaping them. Wherever I go, whatever I do, wave after wave of strong, pungent perfumes engulf me as people pass by. I can't always hold my breath waiting for the worst onslaught to dissipate, or people will begin to wonder why I turn purple every time they stop to talk. No, I can only yearn for the good old days when people smelled like people, not perfume factories. A perceptive nose could easily detect a person's occupation – farmer, blacksmith, fisherman, lumberjack. Every trade had its lingering qualities, but the most poignant scents were those that clung to the hands of a rural homemaker.

I can remember climbing up on my mother's knees when her apron smelled like wood smoke from the old kitchen stove. And depending on the moment, the day, or even the season, her hands might smell like sweet mixed pickles or steamed cabbage or cured hams, fresh raspberries or chocolate cake, or even a mixture of warm, sweet milk and hay as she came in from the barn. This was all brought home to me again last Sunday when we were sitting in church and our youngest fellow whispered, "Your hands sure smell good."

I absentmindedly agreed, thinking he had paid me a compliment for wearing hand lotion.

"They smell," he said, "like Sunday dinner – roast beef and onions."

Just as the aroma of certain food indicates our involvement with it, there are telltale signs that manifest our proximity to Christ. The world, however, is not greatly impressed by pungent words of judgment or flattered by an overload of pious sentiment. What appeals most is the subtle perfume of the fruit of the Spirit (Galatians 5:22), that mellow fragrance of love, peace, and joy that emanates from every Christian who walks in close fellowship with the Lord. Without even being aware of it, little deeds of kindness, the works of our hands, often generate a more positive response than an overpowering witness "poured on" at every occasion.

Rise: Read 2 Corinthians 2:14-16.

Shine: Is there a quality in your life that people find repulsive because you come on "too strong"? Seek God's help in toning it down into a pleasing aroma for Him.

Dealing with stark reality

And He said, "Who told you that you were naked?"
Genesis 3:11a

I never cease to marvel at how quickly kids develop a sense of modesty. In fact it doesn't even "develop". It just appears out of nowhere like some phantom thing come to haunt them forever after. And you never know when it may strike. One day Junior is strolling stark naked down the hallway, completely oblivious of that missing dimension which makes him socially acceptable – namely, clothes. By the very next morning, he has turned into a self-conscious puritan who shrieks in protest if anyone so much as brushes past the doorknob while he is getting dressed.

It is all very frustrating for a young mother. For months she has had to brace herself against the embarrassment

81

of Junior's hobbling out of the bathroom with his pants down around his ankles, innocence his only defense against the shock waves rippling among the Sunday guests. Or come sweltering summer's day, she may look out just in time to see a familiar little bare bottom disappearing down the street, a scattered trail of size-two clothing left behind. Hot and embarrassed, she immediately gives chase, much to the delight of her toddling streaker and chuckling neighbors.

And then suddenly, Junior discovers modesty. The bathroom door is no longer left wide open but shut firmly and *locked*. The bedroom is off limits unless mother first knocks. And no more barging in on bath night to check elbows and ears.

From that point on, life at home is difficult at best and trips to the doctor all but impossible – so many people intruding on one small boy's modesty and he absolutely frustrated trying to preserve his privacy.

Mother may as well admit it. Junior is growing up.

Spiritual growth can be observed in much the same way. Despite the best of teaching, a new believer may exhibit little or no Christian conscience immediately following his conversion. Blissfully unaware that his conduct is creating shock waves among the saints, he leaves behind him a lengthening trail of doubts, much to the chagrin of fellow believers and the smug satisfaction of snide skeptics.

And then, quite aside from the frustrated efforts of

concerned Christians trying to counsel him from the *outside*, the Holy Spirit *inwardly* convicts him about the disgrace of a Christian testimony naked of good works. From that point on, he seeks to be clothed in deeds of righteousness.

People from his former way of life may make it difficult at best and all but impossible at worst, but one thing is certain: the young Christian who is conscientious about his Christian commitment need never be ashamed to meet his God.

Rise: Read 2 Corinthians 5:1-10.

Shine: Wherever you go, remember that good deeds and exemplary behavior are always appropriate dress for the Christian.

Plunging in

May the flood of water not overflow me.
Psalm 69:15a

$\mathcal{J}$ finish washing an enormous stack of dishes and pull the plug as usual. Nothing happens. Instead of swirling down the drain with a familiar "guggle," the dishwater refuses to budge. I stand there pondering the dilemma while bits of soggy coleslaw float around the surface and the grease forms a ring around the sink.

My plumbing experience is somewhat limited. If I recall correctly, the toddler in the family once unwound a goodly portion of toilet paper and tried to flush it away before I caught him. On that occasion I had to resort to the old plunger routine to speed things on their way. Another time the water draining from the bathroom sink seemed unduly sluggish, and I remedied the problem by removing a hair clog with a bent coat hanger. Two predicaments do not a plumber make, however.

Still, it doesn't hurt to investigate. I get down on my hands and knees and peer under the sink. One thing is certain. I have to clean out the cupboard in order to reach the pipes.

Having done that, there is no use putting all that stuff back on the shelves without exercising the little plumbing expertise I do possess. With flash-light and pipe wrench I boldly set to work.

Suddenly the connection loosens and a torrent of stagnant dishwater bursts through the dam, inundating the lower shelf and surging out across the kitchen floor.

At least the sink is empty.

What's more, I have located the source of trouble – a plastic straw crumpled crosswise in the drain trap. Kneeling there in the deluge while reassembling the pipes, I keep telling myself I am not really a failure. An expert plumber just has a neater way of doing things.

Number one, he thinks before he acts. I should have reinserted the sink stopper before loosening the connection. A plumber who mops the kitchen floor with the dishwater does not command much respect from his peers.

There are times when my Christian walk slows to a standstill and I sit there pondering my dilemma while bits of self-pity float to the surface and bad attitudes congeal around the edges. I am not the most encouraging person at the best of times, and certainly not when it comes to self-examination. Still, it does not harm to evaluate my circumstances.

What is creating this stagnant state of spirituality? There is no limit to the supply of living water flowing *in*. But am I giving *out*? Or is something hindering me from serving the Lord – a plugged schedule, twisted priorities, hidden faults?

In my anxiety to remedy the situation, I have to stop and *think* before plunging headlong into unfamiliar service. No, I may not be a failure, but more established Christians have a less impulsive way of accomplishing the same goals. An overenthusiastic novice who bumbles in beyond his depth does not command much support from the veterans lining the shore.

Rise: Read Psalm 69:13-17.

Shine: Do you get the impression you are "in over your head" in some particular area? Exercise humility. Withdraw where necessary, and think before you act.

Blessed memories

Having eyes do you not see? And having ears,
do you not hear? And do you not remember?
Mark 8:18

Friend Hubby had a day off from work not long ago, so I took advantage of a rare opportunity and got him downstairs to help me clean the storage room.

It was like stepping backward in time.

We looked through boxes of musty books that had never known the glare of fluorescent lighting. In an old trunk that reeked of mothballs we discovered everything from outdated nickels to baby bootees to autograph books signed by school pals of the dark ages.

But it was the songbooks that provided the most fun. "Once in the dear dead days beyond recall" friend Hubby had been a music teacher. Lo and behold if he didn't find some of his old voice exercises, which he began to practice right on the spot. I hastily rummaged through the rest of the box in search of something to offset the misery. And that's how snatches of his operatic arias interspersed with my shaky renditions of "Home on the Range" came to escape up the stairwell where, high on the third step, the surly old tomcat was switching his tail in obvious annoyance.

The teenager coming home from school was about to reprimand us for going senile when among the cobwebs he spied a tarnished old tuba of postwar vintage. "Hey, I remember that thing! I wonder if I can still play it."

And he let go a "blat" that shook the floor joists and lifted the tomcat straight up from his stairstep podium.

We did not get much accomplished that day as far as cleaning up the storage room, but we certainly had a good time rearranging old memories.

Despite the advaces in technology, the storage capabilities of the human brain are still beyond comprehension. A touch, a taste, a smell, a sound, a sight, can trigger off a host of memories, each with an accompanying emotional impact and personal reaction. I believe that is why the Bible admonished us to remember – to "remember the days of old" (Deuteronomy 32:7), "to remember the Lord" (Nehemiah 4:14), to remember "His wonders ... His marvels" (Psalm 105:5). Nor are we to forget our faults (Genesis 41:9), our former way of life (Ephesians 2:11), and the influential faith of godly ancestors (2 Timothy 1:5).

But the memory that should rekindle the brightest song

in our hearts should be the memory of our salvation, the time when we accepted Jesus Christ as our personal Savior. The experience may have been as emotionally moving as a beautiful operatic aria or as humble as "Home on the Range," but whether certain or shaky, our commitment touched the heart of God. Reminiscing about His faithfulness through a clear personal testimony is a good way to reach the ears of those around us. As for the surly skeptic who, like the tomcat, looks down at you with obvious annoyance, try to take him by surprise and lift him – straight up the golden stairs!

Rise: Read 1 Corinthians 14:7-9.

Shine: Write out your testimony, showing clearly the picture of your life "before" and "after". Notice how you draw upon memories. Make this an important consideration in your approach to others.

Feeding the faint

*And let us not be weary in well doing, for in
due season, we shall reap, if we faint not.*
Galatians 6:9, KJV

There is nothing whatever as debilitating as the flu. If
the Communists wanted to immobilize the entire country,
they need not waste research on exotic germ warfare.
They would just need to turn loose a couple of prolific
flu bugs and let nature take its course. The entire
population would grind to a halt, and the country could
be overtaken without a protest.

Then again, maybe not. There is always that one
courageous soul in every household who manages to
retain his appetite and uses it as a lever to pry up the
bedridden, the old "how-do-you-expect-me-to-get-
better-if-you-don't-feed-me?" weapon.

If it happens to be the breadwinner of the family who
is perishing from hunger, you feel a certain patriotic

obligation to supply him with ammunition in his courageous stand against the enemy. And so you make the effort, and what an effort it is! Your head is light and your feet are heavy and your stomach churns and your back aches, but you hobble on out to the kitchen where stacks of dirty dishes are waiting to greet you and the table hasn't been wiped since you took to bed three days ago. Taking a good long swig of cough syrup and a couple of pain killers, you brace yourself against the stove and begin making supper.

An agonizing hour later, weak-kneed and glassy-eyed, you take your patient his tray. The last thing you remember is seeing him sitting up in bed looking fit as a fiddle. That's when you collapse.

There should be a medal for cooks who perform outstanding service in times of germ warfare.

Although certain heroic measures of that sort may be overlooked here on earth, I believe God in heaven is more conscientious. Scripture tells us plainly in Ephesians 6:12 that we are engaged in spiritual warfare. If the enemy wanted to immobilize Christianity he would not need to devise any aggressive scheme. He need only encourage a sense of apathy and let human nature take its course. "Evil prevails," someone has said, "when good men do nothing."

In the midst of our mass indifference, however, there are those inspiring Christians who, despite opposition, ridicule, and physical limitations feel a certain obligation to lead and feed and teach the lagging soldiers. When they finally collapse, when the Last Post is played for a former pastor or Bible teacher, we realize that much of the credit for our own victorious Christian living goes to their unflinching efforts on our behalf. Little wonder they will receive a "crown of righteousness" on heaven's "Decoration Day."

Rise: Read 2 Timothy 4:1-8.

Shine: Is there a certain person in your life who has rallied you to greater heights of spiritual growth? Tell him so, either by phone or letter or in person. He may be getting "weary in well doing," and you can encourage his heart.

Spontaneous results

I will call for the corn, and will increase it.
Ezekiel 36:29, KJV

Whenever the family smells popcorn they flock to the kitchen like sparrows to a bird feeder, twittering about the old tin soup pot I use as a popper. It's worn a gauge thinner from being agitated over a red-hot element, and the remains of stubborn kernels of corn are cremated black in the bottom, but it works like a charm. When not jostling along on a camping trip, the old popping pan sits under the kitchen sink, ready for action at a moment's notice.

I never know when popcorn fever may strike – in the middle of a family gathering in summer, on a lonesome rainy night in fall, or when a blizzard is howling around the eaves in January.

Best to be prepared. Friend Hubby makes regular trips to a rural town whose inhabitants have not yet learned that good things come in small packages. They bag their popping corn in twelve-pound sacks, which friend Hubby lugs home two at a time.

I have a recipe file bulging with ways to sugar popcorn, and I triple every recipe. I sometimes fear the Crackerjack people will get wise to the competition and insist I buy a business license.

If so, I shall have to prove to them that my popping factory is really quite primitive – the old tin soup pot with the spool knob bolted on the lid, a scorched oven mitt, a warped stove element, some oil and corn, and a bit of luck. For personnel I appoint somebody with good nerves to fan the smoke detector with a tea towel, because every time I step up production, the alarm goes off. Meanwhile friend Hubby stands by with two wooden spoons to stir the boiling syrup into the popcorn at just the right moment.

The results are infinitely more satisfying that anything money can buy, each sweet tender morsel a prize in itself.

And for those who have never tasted it, the rewards of Christian service are infinitely sweeter than anything the world has to offer. People may twitter and chirp about the simplicity of the gospel, and yet there are those who cannot resist its appeal. Believers the world over still flock to church to "gobble up" the gospel message.

In comparison to the world, our methods may seem primitive, but they are personal – vessels wholly committed to serving the Lord, the glow of warm fellowship, the anointing oil of the Spirit of God, and dedicated people on standby to fan the power of prayer. Meanwhile, "all things work together for good to those who love God, to those who are the called according to His purpose" (Romans 8:28).

Just as hard little kernels of corn pop into tender white morsels, hardened souls have been known to explode into vibrant Christian workers. "O taste and see that the Lord is good. How blessed is the man who takes refuge in Him" (Psalm 34:8).

Rise: Read Ezekiel 36:26-28.

Shine: It is frustrating to work with people who lack initiative, but have you examined your *own* attitude lately? Genuine enthusiasm in an indifferent world is like hot buttered popcorn on a cold night – few can resist it!

A surprise in store

You do not know what your life will be like tomorrow.
James 4:14

$\mathcal{F}$or the first time in twenty-three years, friend Hubby was going to be away from home overnight. As I crawled into bed in my flannel pajamas with the hot-water bottle, the only encouraging thing I could think of was the fact that I could sleep in tomorrow. None of this "rise 'n' shine at 6:00 A.M." philosophy that makes naturally lazy people like myself feel guilty. Tomorrow I could sleep in as long as I wanted and be served breakfast in bed at that.

The kids had insisted.

The long cold night dragged wearily by, and somewhere in the wee hours of the morning I finally fell asleep. At 6:30 A.M. the tomcat couldn't stand the silence any longer. With no master to keep him company at breakfast, he started to yowl. I finally padded down he hallway in my slippers to rescue him from the misery of his own company. He rather liked the idea of coming back to bed with me, but he purred so loudly I couldn't go back to sleep.

One hour. Two. Between the tomcat's purring and my stomach growling, the bedroom sounded like a zoo.

At last I could hear the kids whispering about breakfast possibilities. When the printed menu finally arrived I politely declined the "chocklut serup with pancakes" and settled for "Toste with scrambulled eggs and kofee."

Although I was vaguely aware that there was some confusion surrounding the actual preparation procedures, in due course my breakfast tray arrived. When I tried to stir the coffee, I noticed it offered some resistance to the spoon. Not until I reached the half inch of sludge in the bottom of the cup, however, did I realize that my youthful chefs had used flour instead of coffee whitener. Looking at their innocent beaming faces, I suddenly realized that those lovely scrambled eggs and that hot buttered toast had made me feel so full I just couldn't drink another sip of coffee. Thank you just the same. Yes, of course, breakfast in bed was just delightful!

There are experiences in life that turn into memorable occasions for the wrong reasons. Despite careful planning, perhaps you find yourself suddenly left alone in a responsible position. The very thought of it leaves you cold. Determined to make the best of it, however, you struggle on through the weary hours, only to have the wails of a lone dissident grate on your nerves at an inopportune moment in time. Afraid of awakening further protests, you hush complaints as best you can.

The burden grows tiresome indeed.

At last there are whispered rumors that help is on the way. Ten chances to one it will be somebody with twice as much enthusiasm as ability, who creates a bigger mess than he finds, but whose sincere effort to be of assistance somehow compensates for all his bumbling mistakes. What promised to be a disaster has been redeemed by the innocent childlike faith of one of God's children.

Rise: Read Philippians 2:1-4.

Shine: Has someone recently done her best to help you out of a depressing situation? Show her your appreciation.

Premature pride?

You cannot make one hair white or black.
Matthew 5:36

When our first boy was born with a good thatch of hair, I was naive enough to feel smug about it. I mean, the Barkman baby just stood out head and shoulders above all those smooth little billiard balls down in the nursery.

A year later I would have gladly exchanged him for any one of them.

Hair grows, you see, and in no time at all he looked like a sheep dog in diapers. For his first birthday we had to buy him a set of clippers and give them to him three months early. That's when "The Ordeal" began.

He did not like getting his hair cut. He wiggled and squirmed and whined and stuck his lollipop in my eye and swiveled his head around like it was attached to a universal joint. So I'd give him a mirror to watch the proceedings, and he'd promptly go into hysterics because he thought I was going to decapitate him with a pair of thinning shears.

I probably spent more money in bribes than if I had taken him to the barber.

"If you want to go to the zoo, you'd better sit still!"

"If you want some candy, you'd better hold your head up!"

"If you want –"

If he had wanted to get his hair cut in the first place it would have helped, but he no sooner learned to accept the physical discomforts than he started to dread the social consequences.

"Aw, c'mon, Mom! All the kids are gonna tease me."

"Aw, c'mon, Mom! All the kids are gonna laugh at my ears."

"Aw, c'mon, Mom! All the kids –"

To let him tell it, he'd have to wear his baseball cap twenty-four hours a day to spare himself the awful humiliation. Long before he reached adulthood I had learned to regret the pride I had once taken in that beautiful head of hair. Making a quick comparison in the nursery, I had glowed with the smug pride of ownership quite apart from the realities that lay ahead.

Time passes, you see, and what may seem to be an endearing source of joy right now can become a literal headache a few months down the road.

That new house that seems so perfect now will mean

recurring mortgage payments for years to come. That new car will require a surprising amount of upkeep. Trimming the budget and cutting financial corners may fall within your optimism at the moment, but other factors may enter in to aggravate the situation later on. In retrospect, you may wonder, as I do, how you could have been so short-sighted in the first place.

Surely if the Lord numbers all the hairs on our heads, He will provide for us in His own good time. Not knowing what lies in the future, we need to weigh matters realistically and prayerfully as we take on added responsibilities.

Rise: Read Luke 14:28-33.

Shine: To "give up" all your possessions is to relinquish them to the will of the Lord. In making a hasty decision we rarely take time to "consider the cost" in terms of the kingdom of God. Before making your next big decision, therefore, examine your motives and avoid jumping to premature conclusions.

Reducing the idols

Whose god is their appetite.
Philippians 4:19

After my snickering for years about people going on diets, the middle age spread finally caught up to me at the doctor's office. He looked at the scale, peered over his glasses, and told me to lose twenty pounds. Just like that.

All of a sudden his lean frame wasn't tall and slim anymore. He looked positively bony – a living skeleton. I certainly didn't want to go rattling around like *that*.

Ten pounds maybe?

Nope. Fifteen for sure, depending upon my bone structure.

I assured him I had very big bones. He looked at my long skinny fingers.

"Mrs. Barkman, I believe you must lose at *least* twenty pounds." His emphasis on "least" implied that it could actually be more, so I promptly stopped pleading my case.

By his own admission he had just conceded that my fingers were slim. Now to concentrate on the rest of me would be the problem.

The first major hurdle was to pass the candy counter on the way out of the medical mall. Can you imagine? Millions of calories stacked right up there to test your will power not five minutes after you'd been told to lose twenty pounds. I decided to look the other way. There was a lunch counter on *that* side: "Afternoon special – strawberry shortcake with whipped cream!" I closed my eyes, headed for the exit, and ran into a pillar.

From that day to this I have been conscious of food. The world is polluted with it. Every newspaper is loaded with recipes, every magazine filled with fattening menus. Just when I am enjoying a TV program, somebody spoils it with a high-calorie commercial. In spite of all the temptations, the scale is slowly, slowly edging downward, but for the first time in my life I have come to see what a priority we place on food here in the Western world. The need for it cannot be disputed, but the emphasis placed upon it bears close resemblance to idolatry.

In Hebrews 12:1 the King James Version likens Christianity to a race in which we are advised to lay aside "every weight, and the sin which doth so easily beset us." Just as physical weight can handicap us and become a hindrance to our health, there are spiritual encumbrances that can impede our progress as well. We may try to justify a quick temper, a bad habit, and flabby morals, but they are not conducive to a healthy Christian witness. Nor will the temptation to indulge simply disappear. The more we try to refrain, the greater will be the struggle. It is only as we recognize the *source* of our problem and approach it from a different perspective – from God's viewpoint – that we see ourselves as we really are.

Rise: Read 1 Corinthians 10:6-14.

Shine: Have certain priorities, goals, or values that are handicapping your Christian witness crept into your life? What would be your reaction if they were pointed out to you? Instead of taking offense, take the initiative, and accept God's directions in refusing anything that adds negatively to your Christian image.

Crossing the line

For our citizenship is in heaven.
Philippians 3:20a

It was the longest line-up I had ever seen at a Canadian customs office. Cars stretched out single-file across the North Dakota prairie like the old-time wagon trains. This time we weren't being ambushed by hostile natives. We were being inspected by punctilious customs officers, one car at a time. Stop and go. Stop and go. We probably used more gasoline edging up to the international border than crossing the entire state.

Time must have grown exceedingly heavy on the hands of would-be smugglers. Having no such guilt to burden my conscience, I could observe how others passed their time. Some took the opportunity to houseclean their ashtrays. Others strolled around their vehicles looking for imaginary flats. A woman expended a half roll of film taking snapshots of her sons leaning against the

Canada United States border sign. An American in a house trailer brewed yet another pot of coffee.

At one point an impatient driver at the back of the line broke ranks and drove right through customs without stopping to report. The siren blew, officers gave chase, and he was meekly herded back to face the consequences. A second car that tried the same stunt was foiled at the pass and forced to go all the way back to the end of the line.

Eventually a white Cadillac drove up, all pride and prestige, boldly fendering its way into the lineup wherever bumpers weren't virtually touching. In no time at all he had barged right up to customs while the rest of us courteously waited our turn. It was with great satisfaction, therefore, that we saw him being pulled over for more detailed inspection.

When we were finally cleared and on our way, the white Cadillac was still being held for scrutiny, a frowning customs officer probing the depths of its gaping trunk. With its doors drooping open, it looked like a humiliated hen in a rainstorm.

In retrospect I began to liken that experience to its spiritual parallel. Uncertain prospects of the coming judgment day must grow heavy indeed upon the minds of those who have not made their peace with God. Burdened by a guilty conscience, they spend the passing time engaged in irrelevant pursuits. Some become fanatical perfectionists.

Others vainly look for some excuse to delay the inevitable. For some the borderline between life and death takes on a morbid fascination. Others appear totally indifferent.

But there are those individuals who are presumptuous enough to think that they are the exception, that their pride and prestige here on earth somehow entitle them to special privileges. They believe they can elbow their way past the truths of Scripture and somehow bribe God into granting them an exemption. Yet Christ said, "I am the way, and the truth, and the life; no one comes to the Father, but through Me" (John 14:6). Only on His terms, at His time, can we cross from life to death and go home to heaven with a clear conscience.

Rise: Read 1 Timothy 6:6-11.

Shine: It is a sobering thought to know that we are each held accountable for what we do: "Inasmuch as it is appointed for men to die once and after this comes judgment" (Hebrews 9:27). Remember that verse the next time you are tempted to skirt the rules and smuggle some situational ethics into Christianity.

Singing I go?

Like a sparrow in its flitting ...
Proverbs 26:2

I was standing in front of the fresh produce counter at the supermarket when "twitter, chirp!" – a bird flew over my head. *Can't be! I must be hearing things.* Canned bird calls, maybe? Oranges, pineapples, bananas, songbirds – the perfect tropical atmosphere, right here in your friendly neighborhood supermarket. Are there no limits to sales gimmicks and sound effects?

Swoosh, chirp – there it went again. I was *not* just hearing things; I was seeing them. A real sparrow was careening around above my head.

Now what does an ordinary sparrow *do* in a supermarket? Pretty much the usual, I would assume, keeping a wary eye above my head. Amused customers grinned as they watched the sparrow flit from sign to sign. Peanut butter – "cheap, cheap!" Crackers – "cheap, cheap!"

Corn flakes – "cheap, cheap!" For its size, the sparrow was doing a great job of advertising.

A red-faced produce manager stood by helplessly, no doubt dreading what the sanitation inspector might discover. The sparrow was not worried. It just kept up a flying commentary on current prices, while customers and cashiers alike bobbed and ducked to stay out of its path.

Soon one of the packing boys was on its trail with an enormous fishing net he had borrowed from a sporting goods store nearby. Bit by bit he coaxed the bird toward the exit and out into the mall. From there a schoolboy willingly took up the chase. Round and round they went, until the sparrow eventually flew against a glass door. As the boy cautiously walked up to see if it was hurt, the exit door opened automatically and the sparrow walked out as if it had shopped for birdseed at this supermarket every day of its life.

That bird reminded me of believers who turn up in unexpected places of business, much to the chagrin of employers who are rather embarrassed to hear and see a cheerful Christian attitude ringing out above the noise of the cash registers. If you are a Christian doing a creditable job, you cannot really be banished from the scene in one bold scoop. You may be harassed. You may become flustered, but as long as your work habits are above and beyond reproach, you cannot too easily be snared.

There may come a time, however, when the light of godly discernment will guide you toward the exit. Your contribution to this particular place of employment could be coming to an end. Providing you have not compromised your Christian standards, you can walk out the door with dignity, knowing that God "will cover you with His pinions, and under His wings you may seek refuge. His faithfulness is a shield and bulwark" (Psalm 91:4).

Rise: Read Matthew 10:27-32.

Shine: Put in a word of Christian hope and cheer wherever you have the opportunity. The most improbable place is where it is likely needed the most.

Soundly reassuring

*Do not despise prophetic utterances. But examine
everything carefully; hold fast to that which is good.*
1 Thessalonians 5:20-21

$\mathcal{P}$redictions of dire things to come is more than
woman's intuition. It is a result of our acute sense of
hearing.

We know, for instance, that the kitchen sink trap is
beginning to clog when the water no longer goes "guggle,
guggle, groink" down the drain. If you pull the plug and
there is an ominous silence, call the plumber. There is
nothing worse than bailing out yesterday's dishwater,
especially when some smart crack on the bucket brigade
asks how come Mom is throwing out all her homemade
soup.

And while the plumber is there, tell him to listen to
the toilet. You've noticed of late it has stopped its
customary gagging spells and started gargling. If he asks

sarcastically whether you want him to prescribe cough syrup or a decongestant, show him the door. He can't even diagnose a sluggish flush by the sound it makes.

Electricians are no better. I have consequently learned not to call a service man when an appliance develops a queer noise. Yesterday it was the refrigerator. The clock was humming, the washer whirring, the kettle gurgling, and the furnace growling, but the fridge sounded more like the monotone note on a bagpipe. I finally pulled the plug to put it out of its misery.

Now what? I decided to prop the flashlight up on the cabbages and take a look inside the thermostat control. I doodled and tinkered quite a while but at last I heard a familiar click. *Aha!* I said to myself. *The missing note in my kitchen symphony.* The menfolk quickly explained it away as a stuck spring, but the fridge has been performing like a virtuoso ever since.

Contrary to what the world believes, predictions of dire things to come are not simply figments of the imagination. Christians who have their ears tuned to Scripture are able to identify with increasing certainty some of the signs that are to precede Christ's imminent return. Skeptics who turn a deaf ear are themselves part of such prophetic fulfillment, according to 2 Peter 3:3-4: "Know this first of all, that in the last days mockers will come with their own mocking, following after their own lusts, and saying 'Where is the promise of His coming? For ever since the fathers fell asleep, all continues just as it was from the beginning of creation.'"

It may appear that way on the surface, but perceptive Christians are more alert. Notes of discordance on the world scene prompt them to take a closer look at Bible prophecy. As current events "click" into place, they have the assurance that everything is under control. God is running His world in tune with His own timetable.

Rise: Read Matthew 24:3-27.

Shine: For those who are distressed by current events, the only peace to be found is in Jesus Christ. Extend the gospel *now* before it is too late.

Traveling temptations

*All things are open and laid bare to the
eyes of Him with whom we have to do.*
Hebrews 4:13b

Somewhere in the tourist handbook there must be a
law stating that the amount of junk that accumulates in
the back window of a car is in direct proportion to the
distance traveled.

At the beginning of the trip everybody is super-
organized. There is a suitcase for everything, and
everything is in its suitcase. The maps are in the glove
compartment, the thermos of coffee is at your feet, the
snacks are all tidily tucked into a box.

You haven't driven fifty miles when you realize you
have no place to put the gum wrappers and the candy
papers and the orange peels, so you jam all you can into
every available ash tray, and whatever is left goes into
an empty cracker box in the back window.

The sun is getting warm, so one by one everybody sheds their jackets, and these go back to keep the cracker box company. Then you stop for lunch and Junior insists on taking along the hamburger containers because he thinks they'd make good puppets. Guess where he tosses them.

By now the countryside is beginning to look interesting, so at the next stop all the camera paraphernalia is made ready. Then the maps have to come out, and by and by the souvenirs start accumulating – all in the back window. Five hundred miles later you have a McGee's closet right out there where every passing motorist can see it. Let friend Hubby step on the brake pedal too suddenly, and a mountain of junk tumbles onto the back seat, inundating the passengers under a landslide of cameras, books, magazines, jackets, Kleenex, jawbreakers, baseballs, toys, sunglasses, cups, pillows, souvenirs, and the cracker box full of garbage.

Don't laugh! It is just as easy, but somewhat less obvious, to collect rubble in our Christian walk. Every time someone "chews us out" we stick the gum wrappers of resentment back in the far corner of our memory. Someone sweet-talks us into compromise, and we wrap it up as a bad experience and toss it out of our conscience. One by one we peel off our principles. The heat is on, so we shed our "cloaks of righteousness." Before long we start treasuring up the souvenirs of success – money, prestige, power – all out there where everybody can see them.

But sometimes God slams on the brakes, and as life screeches to a stop, we discover our Christian testimony has been buried in an avalanche of irrelevant values. Our intentions of keeping a spotlessly clean testimony right from the start have been littered by carelessness along life's road. Humiliated by the mess, we have to ask God to help us clean it up.

Rise: Read Matthew 10:5-12.

Shine: Keeping the purpose of your spiritual pilgrimage in mind, think safety: clean up the accumulation of worldly values that is blocking your spiritual vision. God's people are to travel light.

Slowed by necessity

There is an appointed time for everything.
Ecclesiastes 3:1

$\mathcal{N}$ever go to the supermarket on the eve of a long weekend. The prices are all jacked up and the air conditioner turned down so you have to grab what you want before your rheumatism starts protesting and your brain goes numb from the chill. There are never enough shopping carts to go around, so you begin piling your purchases on a ten pound bag of briquets. As you labor up and down the aisles your arms slowly disengage from your shoulder sockets and your varicose veins bulge blue from the effort of it all. And just when you have your load all nicely balanced, someone will thoughtlessly butt you from behind with a shopping cart.

You have your mind set on steak, but this being barbecue season, the butcher is laughing to see such sport, and the price of beef has jumped over the moon.

You wrangle your way into the crowd and round up a stray pack of chicken instead.

And then it's into a long line-up at the check-out. You stand there with arms loaded, shifting your weight from one foot to the other while the chicken juice seeps down your front, and the carton of ice cream starts to dribble, and the lady in front of you argues with the cashier over the price of lettuce. Judging from her meticulous concern for prices you might think she is loaded with ready cash. But no. You wait while she writes out a check and the cashier confirms her credit and the manager is called all the way from the back office to scribble his OK. All the while your arms ache, and your back breaks, and nobody, but nobody, is in the least bit of hurry.

Trying to beat the crowds at a supermarket is like running ahead of God. It costs in the long run, and yet I never learn.

When the grace I need to carry me through seems unavailable, I am inclined to forge foolishly ahead on my own, stretching my human resources to the limit. My efforts are so precariously balanced they are apt to topple at any moment. Even though my goals seem within easy reach, other people continually walk away with the promotions I seek, and I reluctantly settle for second best.

Even at that, I have to pay the price, agonizing over the slow advancement, losing patience with people who impede my progress. All in all, life seems frustratingly slow when it comes to accommodating *my* desires.

If I could only learn to rely upon God's timing, my schedule would be half as hectic, the challenges far more pleasant, the achievements gratifying. Compared to the turmoil of impulsively grabbing what I want in a crowded supermarket, waiting on God is like falling in line at the express lane on a slack day.

Rise: Read Ecclesiastes 3:1-9.

Shine: Slow down! The goals you seek will still be there tomorrow. If not, who needs them?

Appropriating truth

*Thy words were found and I ate them, and Thy words
became for me a joy and the delight of my heart.*
Jeremiah 15:16

When the neighborhood gang came trooping in for a drink of orange juice, there was a new face in the crowd. I happened to be mixing bread, and he sidled over to where I was working and looked into the bowl.

"Yuck! What's that stuff?"

"That's going to be bread."

Highly amused that I should try to fool him like that, he started to giggle. "Hey, Glen! Your mom says she's makin' bread outta this stuff!"

"So what? She makes it lotsa times."

The stranger's eyes widened in disbelief. "Wow! Is that a magic bowl or somethin'?"

I tried my best to explain about yeast, but he seemed convinced that I was endowed with supernatural powers.

A few hours later he came back to stare in awe at the fresh loaves of bread cooling on the counter, and then he tore off home, no doubt to relate this strange phenomenon to his mother.

She probably dismissed the whole thing as a fantasy. "Johnny, you *know* people do not bake bread in this day and age. Now stop asking me to do the impossible!"

There are Christians who, like Johnny's mother, seem to think some things are outside the realm of their personal capability. They refuse, for instance, to take an obscure passage of Scripture and work it into something meaningful. They admire people who do. They listen week after week to ministers who feed them fresh portions of the Bread of Life. But encouraged to try it on their own through systematic Bible study, they withdraw from the challenge.

Perhaps it is because seeing is believing. To believe that Bible study is beneficial to spiritual growth while at the same time refusing to engage in it reveals a lack of appetite for the Word. Lack of appetite for scriptural truth indicates wrong priorities. Best not to get involved. Bible study just might uncover what is already obvious anyway – the pathetic indifference of many professing Christians to the Word of God.

Spiritual malnutrition does not occur here in the Western world because of lack of Bread. It afflicts Christians who neglect the Bible to the point that they no longer have an appetite for the Word.

Rise: Read Psalm 107:17-22.

Shine: Is the Bible only an occasional snack or the daily sustenance of your soul? The growing Christian needs a well-balanced diet of spiritual nutrition in the form of Bible study, fellowship, and prayer. Get involved, but don't count on "eating out" all the time. Have personal daily devotions in your own home as well.

Mixed allegiance

No one can serve two masters; for either he will hate the one and love the other, or he will hold to one and despise the other. You cannot serve God and mammon.
Matthew 6:24

When I coaxed friend Hubby to nail up a bird feeder some years ago, I never realized the implications. I just thought it would be a nice gesture on my part and visiting birds would offer me some entertainment in return. It hadn't been up a month when a neighbor accused me of setting a death trap. "All those innocent little birds coming to eat and your old tomcat just itching for a pair of sparrow drumsticks! That's not exactly right, you know."

I meekly agreed.

Would she like my tomcat?

No, thank you. She had allergies.

My bird feeder then?

No. Her husband hated sparrows.

She made it clear that smart people don't mix feathers and fur.

My conscience was somewhat eased by the fact that bird-watching was mostly a spectator sport for my tomcat.

The sparrows, however, never let me forget my folly. If I refuse to feed them, endless hours of "chitter, chirp, chitter" grate on my nerves. If *I* try to justify my neglect, *they* try to solicit sympathy, feigning weakness and fluttering to the ground in search of empty husks. If all else fails, they line up along the eaves trough in dismal silence and peer in at my table loaded with food.

I feel like a glutton in a refuge camp.

Making constant provision for my basic sinful nature is like setting up that bird feeder. I think more about the returns than I do about the risks. I may even be offended when "neighboring" Christians of deeper insight point out the spiritual snares involved. My conscience is somewhat eased by the fact that no apparent damage to my Christian walk is occuring, even though the threat exists.

Ultimately, however, I have to cope with the consequences of my actions. More often than not, it is the niggling reminders of my initial choice that produce the most guilt. I may make a commitment to the wrong crowd and feel I should follow through.

Sympathy for their plight may make me reluctant to

withdraw support at a crucial moment in time. Worst of all, I can hardly withstand the awful peer pressure to conform, the accusing expectations heaped upon me in silent ridicule.

The only way I can avoid such dilemmas is to exercise the foresight of Romans 13:14: "Make no provision for the flesh in regard to its lusts." The forces of evil may fly all about me, but I do not have to build bird feeders in my backyard. I do not have to set up unnecessary snares.

Rise: Read 1 John 2:15-17.

Shine: Does a current desire you have originate in God or in the world? Could it endanger someone else's spiritual walk? Even though it may seem to be a harmless diversion, "by sinning against the brethren and wounding their conscience when it is weak, you sin against Christ" (1 Corinthians 8:12).

Immature insistence

Do all things without grumbling or disputing.
Philippians 2:14

*F*riend Hubby came home from work one day expecting to seek asylum in the rec room. As it happened, he nearly stumbled right into a meeting of the "Club."

"What," he demanded, "is all that uproar in the basement?"

"That," I informed him, "is a bunch of ten-year-old boys planning a clubhouse. You might do well to listen in, since it's going to be erected in your back yard."

"Says who?"

"Says the president. He shouted down the plan man, the warrior, and the security guard just so they'd be able to nail the boards to your tool shed."

As the meeting progressed, bits and pieces of conversation reverberated up the stairwell. By piecing things together, we learned that the clubhouse would be eleven feet tall, have six rooms, would utilize the abandoned tree fort as a spy lookout, and be out of bounds to girls unless they brought something to eat. Moreover, all members would operate under a code name and traitors would be extended no mercy whatsoever.

The matter of club dues proved to be somewhat sticky. After a heated discussion in which the security guard threatened to punch the president in the nose (and I had to go down and restore order), the club members decided to raise money selling pizza to their enemies – said pizzas to be done in a sister's toy oven – providing it could be smuggled out to the clubhouse without her knowledge. If intercepted, they would offer her an honorary membership – said privileges of which meant she could attend club meetings without bringing any chocolate chip cookies.

Although we cannot help but smile at the subtle scheming of children, such immaturity is sad when it surfaces among Christians who should have outgrown it.

The story is all too familiar. An individual seeking spiritual refuge may stumble into a crossfire of opposing viewpoints. The basis of such friction usually proves to be insignificant were it not blown all out of proportion by strong-willed individuals having vested interests. The sad part is that there are always those who are more willing to compromise than to adhere to the biblical principles of love and integrity. When that happens, "my

127

way," has taken precedence over "thy way", and man becomes a stumbling block instead of a stepping-stone.

"I will build My church," the Lord declared, and we, His workmen, are to be helpers, not hindrances.

Rise: Read 1 Corinthians 13:1-11.

Shine: What "childish thing" in your life hinders the Lord's work? Grow up! Quit insisting on your own way and give God a chance.